# *TIPS 4 Teens and Young Adults*

(Tidbits to Financial Literacy)

Janice Dingle Hunter

ISBN:
978-1-7331974-0-3

# DEDICATION

This book is dedicated to

sixteen years and older teenagers, college
students and young adults.

I hope this book inspires you to do your best
in life.

# CONTENTS

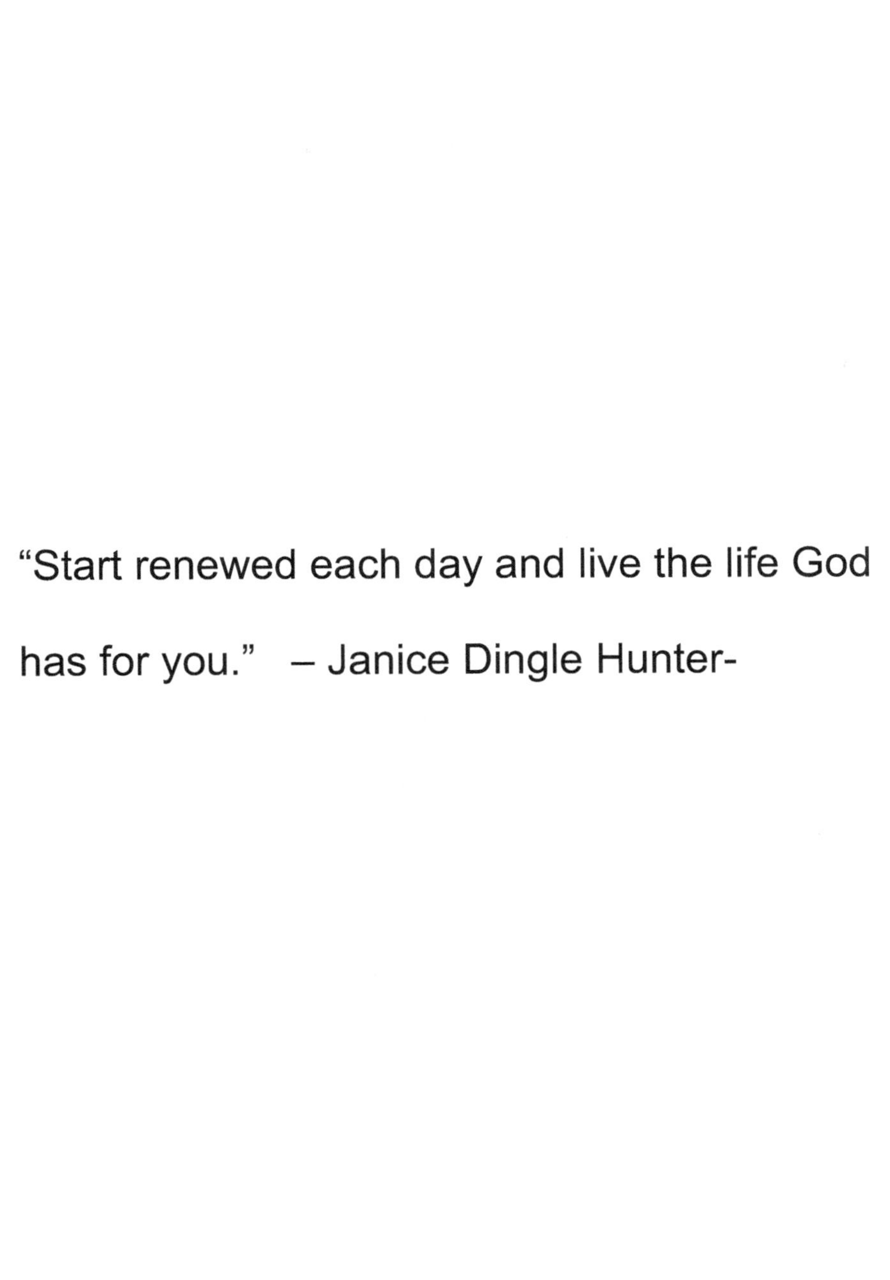

"Start renewed each day and live the life God
has for you."   – Janice Dingle Hunter-

# ACKNOWLEDGMENTS

In memory of my parents who were positive role models in my life.  Thanks for believing in God and for the many sacrifices you made for me to have a better life.  Thanks also for instilling a good work ethic in me, encouraging me to go to college, and to be strong. But most of all thanks for teaching me how to pray and trust in the LORD.

Special thanks to all my sisters who encouraged me to hone my talents, and pursue my dreams.

*Another special thank you to my editor, Jshontista Vann. Thank you for all of your support and hard work. *

# Introduction

Procrastination is a thief of time. Time is one of the most valuable things in existence and in life. Today is present and now and then it is gone, never to return again. Each person has twenty-four hours in a day and what you choose to do with your time is your choice. So therefore, I admonish you, "Do not waste time. Instead learn to manage time wisely."

I would love to go back and be an older teenager or a freshman in college again under one condition. And that condition is to know what I know now. To have the knowledge, education, and experiences I have now. You may wonder why I am saying this especially since I am an adult.

The answer is two-fold: (1) so I would not make the same mistakes and (2) to be in a better financial posture.  You see, you have something most adults wish they had. That something is to be your age.  A lot of adults are thinking, "wow, if I was only young again, I would start saving money and investing sooner." Just think for an adult to be your age and to have the accumulated savings coupled with the compound interest it would make them wealthier than they are today.

Some of you may be wishing you were already an adult so you could make all of your choices without any guidance from your parents and have the freedom to go anywhere you like and so forth.  Listen, please take this sound advice:  do not waste your young years by not going to school and learning all you can in all of your classes and areas of learning.

All learning is important.  But for the purpose of this book I will be primarily focusing on areas dealing with money and money management.

I have wanted to write this book for years but forcing myself to take the time and put my thoughts into words has been quite challenging.  But after getting tired of witnessing what I considered wasteful spending, I felt a sense of urgency to write this book.  I have seen numerous teenagers, college students and young adults in general, as well as in my family, waste a lot of money on buying frivolous stuff.  This is money that they could be saving or with proper guidance investing for the future.

This book is to be used only as a reference to provide or enhance your knowledge about personal finance and money management.  You should consult with a professional financial consultant prior to making any financial or investment decisions.

# Chapter 1: Divine Purpose

When I was a young girl I loved to daydream. I also loved to read books and daydream what it would be like to live in the places that I read about. I would often look out of the window in the side room in our home and I would daydream.

I would day dream about a treasure chest that had lots of treasures and jewels in it. I would day dream that I was a princess and would dream about beautiful castles.

I would daydream that I lived in a beach house directly on the beach and could see the lighthouse and the ocean waves.

I would also day dream often about my grandfather who was a preacher and died

when I was a young girl.  I would imagine
how nice it would be if he was alive and
could spend time with me.  I guess I day
dreamed about my deceased grandfather
because my other three grandparents were
alive and I was able to spend lots of time
with them.  My father's mother lived in the
house next door so I saw her practically
every other day.  My grandmother owned a
small neighborhood store and sold sodas,
cookies, candies, pickles, pig feet, can
sausages, chewing gum, potato chips,
crackers, and other small items.  I would
help her in the store sometimes and helped
her to conduct inventory at the end of each
month.  My mother's parents owned a small
farm in another city.  We visited them at
least twice a week.  I enjoyed spending time
on the farm with my grandparents.  I recall
sitting on the screened in porch with my
grandparents and they would be in rocking
chairs and talking with me.  I enjoyed the
special attention.  My granddad would ask
me questions and would give me coins if I

answered the questions correctly.  He mostly gave me dimes or quarters and told me to save them.  I remember my grandmother cooked on a wood stove and made the best juicy sweet potatoes and homemade biscuits.

My parents took me and my siblings to church on Sundays and we had bible study in our home.  As a result, my faith evolved and I believed in the God of Abraham, Isaac and Jacob.  I also became a born-again believer in the salvation of Jesus Christ at the age of eleven years old.  I am still a Believer and enjoy sharing the good news with others when an opportune time arises.

My parents also taught us how to keep a clean house, how to work hard farming and growing vegetables, and how to treat elders and others with respect.  They also taught us "your word is your bond," meaning do not lie and if you tell someone you are going to do something, do it.  If you cannot do it for whatever reason, inform the person directly as soon as you realize that you cannot do it.

They also taught us the ten commandments (Exodus 20:2-17, KJV) and to live by them. They are as follows:

(1)  Thou shalt have no other gods before me.
(2)  Thou shalt not make unto thee any graven image/idol (i.e., celebrities, T.V., money, relationships, friends, etc.)
(3)  Thou shalt not take the name of the LORD thy God in vain.
(4)  Remember the Sabbath day to keep it holy.
(5)  Honor thy father and thy mother.
(6)  Thou shalt not kill.
(7)  Thou shalt not commit adultery.
(8)  Thou shalt not steal.
(9)  Thou shalt not bear false witness against thy neighbor.
(10) Thou shalt not covet.

I think the greatest thing my parents taught me was how to pray and to trust in

God.  I would hear my parents sing this song often, "I will trust in the Lord, I will trust in the Lord, I will trust in the Lord until I die" etc.  I do not remember the exact name of the song or who wrote the song.  But that stanza in the song became embedded into my memory.  I would also hear them pray each morning and every night.

The taught me and my siblings to pray the Lord's Prayer, (St. Matthew, 6:9-13, KJV) and is follows:

"Our Father which art in heaven, Hallowed be thy name.  Thy kingdom come. Thy will be done in earth, as it is in heaven. Give us this day our daily bread.  And forgive us our debts, as we forgive our debtors.  And lead us not into temptation, but deliver us from evil:  For thine is the kingdom, and the power, and the glory, forever.  Amen".

I grew up with the love to travel and see different places.  I attribute this to my parents taking me and my siblings to visit relatives in different cities and states. Additionally, my younger sister and I would read books about other places. We would discuss them and daydream of living there, especially books about the beach. We would talk about traveling together to see other parts of the world. We aspired to work for the airlines and travel internationally.

I would often daydream of traveling and visiting other countries. That divine purpose became true for me. Whoever would have thought that I would not only travel abroad but to also live and work oversees. I have lived and worked in Europe and Asia. I have visited and seen lots of beautiful castles, just like the ones that I daydreamed about when I was a young girl. I have also traveled to the Holy Land (Jerusalem) and seen many places where Jesus went.

Today I still love to travel, write, talk, interact, and encourage others. I think it is my divine purpose in life.  It is something that I enjoy doing.

Have you ever thought about what you want to become in life?  Becoming an avid adult is cool especially if you are happy and enjoying life.  Inclusive in being happy is having the job, career or business that you are happy doing every day.  I think everyone has a divine purpose in life and when they find it, they are truly happy and fulfilled.

I think fear, doubt, worry and procrastination are some of the greatest hinderances to achieving your goals and dreams and becoming successful in life.  For years I have had to fight the fear of failure when applying for jobs or seeking new ventures.  The "what ifs" always bombarded my mind.  What if this happens or what if they do not like me or what if I cannot do the job.  And doubting in my abilities and worrying became constant obstacles as long as I entertained the negative thoughts.

I had to learn to control the negative thoughts by replacing them with positive ones.  Then I began to speak positive affirmations for my life and for everything I wanted to accomplish.  I still use this technique whenever negativity exalts itself into my thoughts.  The bible tells us that God have not given us the spirit of fear, but of power, and of love, and of a sound mind (2Timothy 1:7, KJV).  The bible is full of positive affirmations to live by.  So, for every circumstance you find yourself in life, search the bible scriptures that are applicable to your situation and begin to think and say what the bible states.  Eventually it will change your beliefs about the matter and you will begin to progress in that area.

Training and managing your thoughts are vital in becoming successful in life.  It is a difficult task to master but can do it and subsequently it becomes easier. The bible also tells us that as a man thinketh in his heart so is he (Prov 23:7, KJV).  So what thoughts are you thinking about yourself? Do you think you can achieve whatever tasks you have set for yourself? If you do not believe in yourself more than likely no one else will. Have you ever been in the company of someone and almost everything they say is negative? And before you know it you begin to speak negative as well. If they feel depressed or not feeling well, before you know it you do not feel well. That is why it is important to watch your thoughts and what you say.

Additionally, we have to pay attention to who our associates are. Who are you socializing with? Do the conversations consist of predominately negative issues or positive ones? Do they uplift or tear down?

Surround yourself with peers who are positive and are seeking to be the best in life. Ask them what are their goals in life. Are they setting goals to contribute good to society? If they are not, you should reconsider having them as your friend. For example, if they are cursing, stealing, lying, cheating, getting drunk, using drugs, selling drugs, disrespecting older people, disrespecting their teachers in school, not going to school, intentionally not working, driving crazy, dressing like a bum, looking and acting wild and foolish and so forth you should avoid having them in your circle of friends. They are hindrances to you becoming successful in life.  You want to socialize or hang out with friends who are setting positive goals and doing good things in life.

Start thinking about what you want to become when you are grown.  A good idea is to start paying attention to what subjects you like in school. What books do you like to read?  What sports do you like to play? What hobbies do you enjoy doing? Sometimes these are clues as to who you are to become.

Start observing other grownups doing their jobs.  Ask them questions such as, "what is your job title", "what do I need to study or major in college to do what you are doing",  "what is the salary range for this type of job",  "do you think this is a good job that will lead to further advancement."

For example, when you go with your parents or by yourself to the bank, post office, hospital, inside companies and so forth, pay attention to the people working there and what they are doing.  Also observe people working outside and what they are doing.

Start reading books and magazines on jobs and careers and what they are about. With the modern computer technology, we have today, you can research it on the internet.  Try to expose yourself to as many career fields as possible and read about them to see if it is something you may want to do.

Research the salaries as well and see how much a person is paid for doing the type of work or service they are doing. Sadly, too many students go to college and study a certain career field only to become dissatisfied when they get a job in it because the pay is lower than what they thought it would be.

Lastly, I suggest you pray and ask God what your divine purpose is and what you are to pursue in life. Seek ye first the kingdom of God and his righteousness and all these things shall be added unto you (ST. Matthew 6:33, KJV). God is the one who gives us the ability to get wealth (Deuteronomy 8:18, KJV).

# Chapter 2: Money

By now I am sure you know what money is and that it is used to buy goods and to pay for services. You have probably also learned the value of money and the more money you have the more you can buy. You may have come to realize the purchasing power of money is a good thing because it buys the digital games, the latest clothes fashions and other trendy things you want. You may also relate to money in terms of the services it pays for such as the hair styles and haircuts you receive, and so forth. However, I want you to realize and begin to utilize the saving power of money because it is a much better thing.

Consequently, in order to save you must have money, and in order to have money, you must work. Not unless you are born into wealth or inherit it. And for most people that is not the case. So do not regret to work and earn money. It is a good thing.

However, what is extremely important is what to do with your money after you work.  For example, you can give it away, you can save it, you can spend it, or you can invest it.  Working and saving your money early in life puts you on the starting path to acquiring wealth.

Lastly, a word of caution when it comes to money.  Always put God first when it comes to money.  Do not fall in love with "the love of money" and let it rule you.  According to 1Timothy 6:10, KJV, the love of money is the root of all evil.  It is okay to have money and to become rich as long as you do not worship it and forget about God, the one who allows you to acquire money in the first place.

So, keep money in its proper perspective.  I suggest you to put God first and pay tithes when you get money. And always be willing to give and help someone in need with a portion of it.  Save, invest and spend accordingly.  Always remember,

money is to be used and not worshipped.
Therefore, put it to good use.

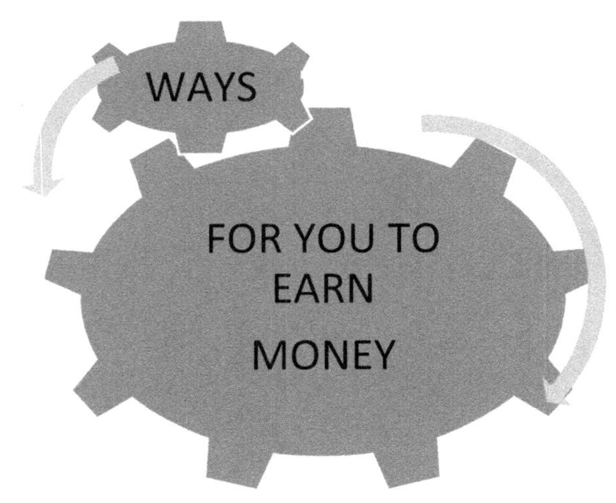


| |
|---|
| PARENT HELPER |
| CAR WASHER |
| LAWN CARE |
| GROCERY STORE CASHIER |
| COLLEGE WORK STUDY JOB |
| GROCERY STORE STOCKER |
| RESTAURANT HOST OR HOSTESS |
| FAST FOOD WORKER |
| TUTOR |
| HOUSE CLEANER |
| BABY SITTER |
| PET SITTER |
| DOG WALKER |
| RECEPTIONIST AT CHURCH |
| YOU TUBER |
| SPORTS ASSISTANT |

| |
|---|
| SELLING FARMERS MARKET VEGETABLES AND FRUITS |
| TEACH MUSIC LESSONS |
| CHURCH MUSICIAN |
| GOLF CADDY |
| MOVIE THEATER WORKER |

# Chapter 3: The Revelation of Tithing and Giving

It is good to get in the habit of tithing when you get money.  When you receive money, I suggest you take 10% of it and pay your tithes to God.  It is God who gives us the ability to get money and he wants us to remember to pay tithes.  "Bring ye all the tithes into the storehouse that there may be meat in mine house and prove me now herewith saith the LORD of hosts if I will not open you the windows of heaven, and pour you out a blessing that there shall not be room enough to receive it" (Malachi 3:10, KJV).

Giving is an important part of enjoying a happy fulfilling abundant life.  You must realize that you are truly blessed if you are a giver.  As a young child, I was taught that it is better to give than receive.  However, I never fully understood the full impact of this statement until after I became an adult.  It became reality to me all at once one day when I was giving some money to a homeless man. I was blessed and able to give.  It is truly better to give than to receive from someone else. I recall my parents were givers and I grew up seeing them give often. I saw them give money, clothes, and food to people they knew as well as to strangers. They grew a big vegetable garden each year and I witnessed them giving away vegetables to others each year.  In the Bible, Jesus states "give and it shall be given unto you; good measure, pressed down, and shaken together, and running over, shall men give into your bosom.  For with the same measure that ye mete withal it shall be measured to you again." (Luke, 6:38, KJV).

You can also give your time by volunteering to help someone in need. Charities or charity organizations are another way you can give. Your parents can help you choose which charitable organization to give to.  Always be a cheerful giver and give from the heart because you want to give.  And God will bless you so much more!

# Chapter 4: The Power of Saving

As a teenager you are not too young to save. And as a college student or young adult you should be saving. As a matter of fact, the sooner you start and really become committed to saving, the better off you will be financially. Your parents are providing all of your basic needs so you should be able to save most of the money that you earn. You can set goals for your savings. For example, you can start saving for your college tuition or your first car.

Your age is the advantage that you have when it comes to saving and investing because you have longer to make your money grow by what is called compound interest. Compound interest makes your money grow faster because interest is calculated on the principal and accumulated interest.  In other words, you are earning interest on your interest.  Due to compound interest, the sooner you start saving and investing the less money you will have to contribute to end up with more money than if you started saving later.  I know you may not fully understand compound interest and investing and that is okay.   The main thing I want you to realize is the importance of saving money and the sooner you start saving the better.  Additionally, the more money you have saved the more you will have to invest wisely or spend.  Your parents can provide you with help and advice or may choose to get help from a professional financial advisor especially if you are able to save a considerable amount of money.

# Chapter 5: Spending

I realize you are going to want to buy the latest digital gadgets, games, fashions and fads.  And you can.  Nevertheless, use wisdom when it comes to spending.  Do not spend ALL of your money when you get paid to purchase these items.

Plan and budget your money so that when you buy these items you can afford them.   You should always prepare a budget before you get paid because it is a good way to track and see where every penny of your money is going.  For example, you take the total amount of what you make and first pay 10% to tithing; then you take 20% for savings; next you take 10% for emergencies; then 5% for charity; and 30% for big purchase spending and 25% for small purchase spending.

An example of an emergency for you may be if your car breaks down. Charity can be given to those in need or charitable organizations of your choice or your parents' choice. Large long-term purchases should be planned spending. For example, perhaps you want to buy a car then you can save for it. Or perhaps you can start saving for your university, college or trade school tuition. Or perhaps it could be for your travel fund in the event you want to travel once you get out of school. Examples of small purchase spending could be that electronic game or cell phone you want, your movie or concert money or the latest clothes fad.

# SAMPLE BUDGET

| | | | |
|---|---|---|---|
| Income | | $500.00 | |
| | | | |
| Tithe (10%) | | | 50.00 |
| Savings (20%) | | | 100.00 |
| Emergency | | | |

| (10%) | | | 50.00 |
|---|---|---|---|
| Charity (5%) | | | 25.00 |
| Long Term (30%) | | | 150.00 |
| Small Purchase (25%) | | | 125.00 |
| Totals: | | $500.00 | $500.00 |

# Chapter 6: Debt the Downer

I can personally attest that debt can make you feel down, and especially excessive debt.  It can make you feel miserable and overwhelmed. Of course, when I was a teenager, I did not have any debt.  But that all changed when I went to college because of student loans and later credit card debt.  After graduating from college, I could not find a job that paid a lot of money and I had accumulated a significant amount of student loan debt.

It was extremely difficult to manage paying basic household debt such as rent, utilities, and transportation fees along with student loan and credit card debt. My parents taught me and all of my siblings to avoid getting into debt.  I recall them saying "debt is easy to get into but hard to get out. Work, save your money and pay cash for what you get." Boy, were they right!  Here I was, not able to pay my debts and not able to eat.  All of my money had to go to paying bills and there was no money left for food. There was not enough money to pay all of the bills in full either.  It is embarrassing to be a grown up and not have the money you need to buy groceries and pay your bills.  It is embarrassing to share this with someone. Thank God for a loving family who helped and gave me money and food.  I remember visiting one of my sisters one day and she gave me a bag full of groceries.  I cried.  Not in front of her though.  She was a real blessing.  Later I was able to find a better paying job and was able to pay down some of my debt to the point I could live a better lifestyle.  It was years later that I learned what I am sharing with you in this book on how to get out of unnecessary debt, save and invest.  As a matter of fact, I am still learning about investing.  It is not easy to choose what to invest in and how to do it. Although I learned a lot in college about finances, I did not understand some of it.  I learned how to do the formulas to get an A or B in the class but living in the real world was so different.  What I learned in the classroom and from reading books was not reality to me until after I began to put it to use.

Debt is a bill or liability that you are responsible for paying.  Avoid getting into debt.   It is best to always use cash or your debit card to pay in full for items that you are buying or services that you want.  And when you graduate from high school do not get caught up in credit card spending. Beware of using charge cards and getting into unnecessary debt.  For example, charging to go out to eat, shopping to buy the latest fads, going to the movies, numerous vacations and so forth.  Charging your credit card to and over the maximum is misuse of it.  Misuse in charging on your credit card can generate high balances, late fees and delinquencies.  Some credit card companies target college students and young people into getting credit cards. These companies have been known to approve and send you numerous credit cards knowing you do not make sufficient money to pay for the use of them.   Do not use a credit card to purchase your goods, services and other unnecessary items.  When you use a credit card it really means you cannot afford what you are buying.  It is not a good thing to be in debt and you cannot pay for it.  It is a miserable feeling and you will be in what I call debt the downer.  If you do decide to use a credit card you are supposed to pay for that debt immediately or prior to thirty days so you will not have to pay accumulated interest on the debt.  And you should never charge your credit card to the maximum amount that you are approved for.

If you cannot pay your debts, your credit worthiness is affected in a negative way which causes your credit score to go down.   This means if and when you need to use credit to apply for a loan from a bank to purchase a house, start a business, or buy a car or some other large purchase, your loan will not be approved to get any credit or approved to get the amount of credit that you want.

So be responsible, and if you decide to use debt, learn how to use it wisely.  Pay your debt before it is due and absolutely no later than the due date.  As an adult, I was blessed to watch a you tube video by Dave Ramsey called "Dave Ramsey Live 7 Baby Steps", you tube video February 19, 2019. If you can I highly recommend you listen to it.  It reminds me a lot of the teachings I received from my parents.  According to Dave Ramsey (2019), "borrowing money and getting into debt puts you at a disadvantage because you are indebted or bound to someone else.  All debt puts you in bondage".  Do not get in the habit of borrowing with the inability to pay your debt in full when it becomes due.  It is so easy to get into debt but it is extremely difficult to get out of.  Lastly, learn how to live a debt free life of unnecessary debt. When you work and make money, make a budget and abide by it.

# Chapter 7: Credit Score

In the future you may have to go to the bank to apply for a mortgage loan to buy a house or apply for a business loan to start your own business.

Having a good credit score will ensure you are approved and will help you qualify for the best interest rates.

Furthermore, having a good credit score is vitally important in our society today and impacts how much you pay for house mortgages, property insurance, car loans, and other loans.

The credit score is broken out as follows:

| CREDIT SCORE | MEANING |
| --- | --- |
| 750 - 850 | Excellent |
| 700 - 749 | Good |
| 650 - 699 | Fair |
| 600 - 649 | Poor |
| 600 - and below | Bad |

Your credit score is reported to three major reporting agencies: Equifax, Experian, and TransUnion. The score ranges from 300 being the lowest through 850 being the highest. Banks and lenders use your credit score to determine your credit worthiness and your ability to repay a loan. The higher your credit score the less risky you are considered for repaying the loan as agreed.

If you are approved for a loan (any kind of loan such as a student loan, car loan, house mortgage loan or a business loan) always be sure to pay it on time and pay the payment amount that is agreed.  If you can pay a little more than the payment amount is good also.  Pay your balance that is due in full every month to avoid paying interest.  If you have a history of making late payments lenders will see you as a bigger risk and your credit score will go down.  Make sure you pay your balance or make a payment at least by the end of the month.  Lenders keep a record of how you pay and it is reported to the credit bureau as a positive report saying you are paying on time as agreed.

If you do not pay on time and by the end of the month and go over 30 days, it is reflected on your credit report as negative and not paying on time.  The longer you go without paying, it is reported to the credit bureaus negatively and as paying late, over

30 days, over 60 days, over 90 days, over 120 days and so forth.

Never use your credit cards to the maximum available credit limit.   It is a good practice to only use no more than 10% to 30% of your total available credit to use. This is called your utilization rate and you want to keep it low so that creditors (lenders) will not see you as a risk.  This utilization rate is also used in computing your credit score each month.  Also, a mistake some young people make is applying for a lot of credit cards or loans. Each time you apply for a credit card or loan it is reflected on your credit report as an inquiry.  Creditors do not like to see a lot of inquiries because you could be seen as a credit risk.

Lastly, when you pay off your credit cards do not close your accounts.  Closing your accounts will lower your credit score. Credit age or history of your accounts is reflected in your credit score.  The longer the history the higher the score.

# Chapter 8: Role Models and Mentorship

Do you have a role model? It is not necessary to have a role model to become successful in life. However, many people choose role models to pattern their life behind or use as a guide as to whom they hope to be like one day. For example, many youths choose an entertainer or a professional athlete that they admire and hope to achieve their successes in life.

If you decide to choose a role model make sure it is a positive role model with a positive image. You can also choose more than one role model. I think having a positive role model can help you to stay motivated as well as help you to achieve your own personal goals. I have read numerous books and heard various lectures on other people and their success stories. Reading and researching how your role model became successful could possibly help you to attain some of your goals by utilizing some of the same steps your role model used if possible.

I think it is good to read books on high achievers and how they became successful. Reading books on others can be extremely enlightening. Many of them had role models they looked up to and followed as well.

A mentor is someone that is more knowledgeable and experienced in an area than you are who is willing to assist you to gain proficiency in that area. Mentorship can be very helpful and rewarding. Having someone to teach you can help you to avoid costly mistakes and can help you to achieve your goals faster.

Always be cognizant when going through life because someone is always observing you.  It can be your teacher in the classroom comparing you to the other students.  It can be your boss at work observing how you do your job in relation to others doing the same job.  It can be a neighbor or a child watching you in your neighborhood.

Imagine if you overheard someone talking about you.  Would you be pleased at what they were saying?  Are you setting a positive example for others to follow?  Are you being a good role model?

**Write a brief paragraph or page on at least 4 role models**

**in your life and WHY you see them as a role model.**

# ROLE MODEL # 1

# ROLE MODEL # 2

46

# ROLE MODEL # 3

47

# ROLE MODEL # 4

48

# GOAL # 1

**DATE FOR COMPLETION:**

**HOW DO YOU PLAN TO ACCOMPLISH THIS GOAL?**

# GOAL # 2

**DATE FOR COMPLETION:**

**HOW DO YOU PLAN TO ACCOMPLISH THIS GOAL?**

# GOAL # 3

**DATE FOR COMPLETION:**

**HOW DO YOU PLAN TO ACCOMPLISH THIS GOAL?**

# GOAL # 4

**DATE FOR COMPLETION:**

**HOW DO YOU PLAN TO ACCOMPLISH THIS GOAL?**

# GOAL # 5

**DATE FOR COMPLETION:**

**HOW DO YOU PLAN TO ACCOMPLISH THIS GOAL?**

# GOAL # 6

**DATE FOR COMPLETION:**

**HOW DO YOU PLAN TO ACCOMPLISH THIS GOAL?**

# GOAL # 7

**DATE FOR COMPLETION:**

**HOW DO YOU PLAN TO ACCOMPLISH THIS GOAL?**

# GOAL # 8

**DATE FOR COMPLETION:**

**HOW DO YOU PLAN TO ACCOMPLISH THIS GOAL?**

# GOAL # 9

**DATE FOR COMPLETION:**

**HOW DO YOU PLAN TO ACCOMPLISH THIS GOAL?**

# GOAL # 10

**DATE FOR COMPLETION:**

**HOW DO YOU PLAN TO ACCOMPLISH THIS GOAL?**

# GOAL # 11

**DATE FOR COMPLETION:**

**HOW DO YOU PLAN TO ACCOMPLISH THIS GOAL?**

# GOAL # 12

**DATE FOR COMPLETION:**

**HOW DO YOU PLAN TO ACCOMPLISH THIS GOAL?**

# GOAL # 13

**DATE FOR COMPLETION:**

**HOW DO YOU PLAN TO ACCOMPLISH THIS GOAL?**

# GOAL # 14

**DATE FOR COMPLETION:**

**HOW DO YOU PLAN TO ACCOMPLISH THIS GOAL?**

# GOAL # 15

**DATE FOR COMPLETION:**

**HOW DO YOU PLAN TO ACCOMPLISH THIS GOAL?**

# Chapter 9: Owning Your Own Business

Have you ever dreamed of owning your own business? Well it is possible and there are many young business owners and entrepreneurs today. Small businesses help to make our economy survive and thrive today.

Several of you will go to college and afterwards will get a job and work for some company or organization. And many of you will become entrepreneurs and own and run your own businesses and companies. Some of you may already have your own business on the internet or otherwise.

Here are some things you may consider. First you will have to decide what type of business you plan to open.  Will it be a service business or a product- based business?  What will be the name of your business?  What will be your target market? Where will it be located? Where will you get the money and resources to start up your business and keep it running?  If you do not have the amount of money needed to start up your business you will have to seek funding from a bank, the Small Business Administration or private investors. Therefore, you will need to have a business plan.  The bank will want to see your business plan prior to giving you a loan. The business plan will show a snapshot of your business and the amount of funding you will need to start up and operate for a specified period of time.  The sample business plan that I am including in this book is a skeletal plan.  In the future if you ever have to prepare a business plan it should be very detailed.  Your business plan should provide a vision for you and anyone who looks at it of where your company is and where it is going.  It is your business roadmap.

On the next couple of pages is a sample business plan.

<u>*NAME OF BUSINESS*</u>

## *Mountainview Senior Care Center*

<u>*BUSINESS LOCATION*</u>

123 Long Street, Bolster, TN 277992

<u>*EXECUTIVE SUMMARY*</u>

Mountainview Senior Care Center is a premier senior care company.  We provide quality senior care services that enables one to feel confident about leaving their parents and love ones.  The Center is designed to be a homelike safe and secure environment. Our vision is that Mountainview Senior Care Center will be the leading center for the Archdale Community and surrounding communities within two years.

## *MISSION*

To provide quality senior care services ensuring safety of each person at all times. Adequate experienced personnel will be hired to ensure proper care of each senior.

## *MARKET ANALYSIS*

Mountainview Senior Care Center is a mid-size facility that services adults from fifty-five to ninety- five years old.  The Center is located in the Archdale Community in Bolster, TN.  The Archdale Community is an upscale community consisting primarily of young married couples aged twenty-two through fifty years old.  Ninety five percent of the couples are educated and employed. Currently there are no other senior care facilities within the Archdale Community and the closest senior care facility is within a fifteen- mile radius.

# TARGET MARKET

An enormous need exists for senior care within our target market.  Our target market consists of seasoned retirees and full-time working adults with aging parents.  This group is forecasted to be fifty nine percent of the total population within the serviced Archdale community.

# MANAGEMENT & ORGANIZATION

Mountainview Senior Care Center has an excellent organizational structure. Minimum essential personnel are currently employed. Open plans are in place to hire additional assistants as needed as the company grows to ensure the safety of each senior.

Current management personnel are as follows:

*Founder & CEO: Carol Davis*

Carol is a Harvard business graduate and has over ten years' experience in leadership and management.  Additionally, she has prior senior care entrepreneurial experience resulting from two previous successful profitable senior care centers.


*Director:  Karla Lewis*

Karla has a Bachelor degree in Healthcare Education.  She has a total of eight years' experience as an administrative assistant and five years as a Senior Care Director at a facility with 125 seniors.


*Assistant Director:  Deborah Withrow*

Deborah has a Bachelor degree in Senior Education and five years senior care activities experience.

# *FINANCIAL PROJECTIONS*

Mountainview Senior Care Center financial projections are enclosed for the current year and the next five years.

**Please note:** I did not enclose financial projections for the Mountainview Senior Care Center.

However, when doing your business plan, it is imperative that you enclose your business financial projections. Financial projections show the numbers for how you expect your business to make an escalating profit from the current year over the course of five years.

# *<u>Chapter 10:</u>*
# *<u>Positive</u>*
# *<u>AFFIRMATIONS</u>*

*On the next few pages are my positive affirmations.  I like to say positive affirmations* because they help me to stay in a positive mood. They also help me increase my faith and to continue to strive towards achieving my goals. I choose to say them out loud and

I try to look in the mirror when I say them.  However, if I am in a hurry, I just read them out loud.  I have said them so much that I've committed them to memory without trying to

memorize them.
I suggest you try
them or create
some positive
affirmations of
your own.

# Positive AFFIRMATIONS (That I Say Out Loud)

I AM A
WINNER

I HAVE THE
WISDOM OF
God

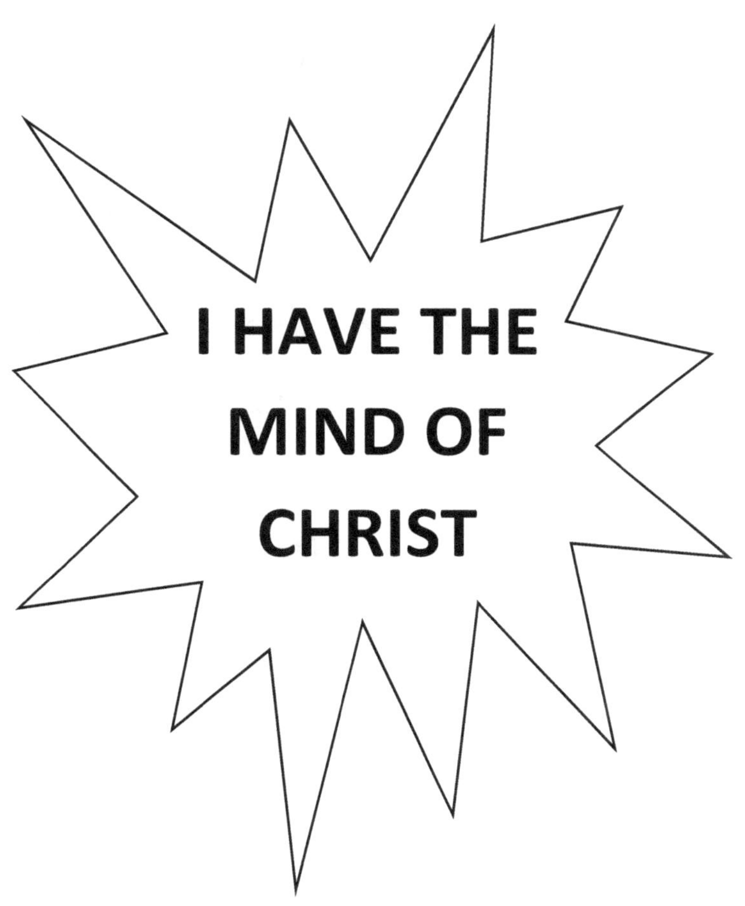
I HAVE THE
MIND OF
CHRIST

NO WEAPON
FORMED
AGAINST ME
SHALL PROSPER

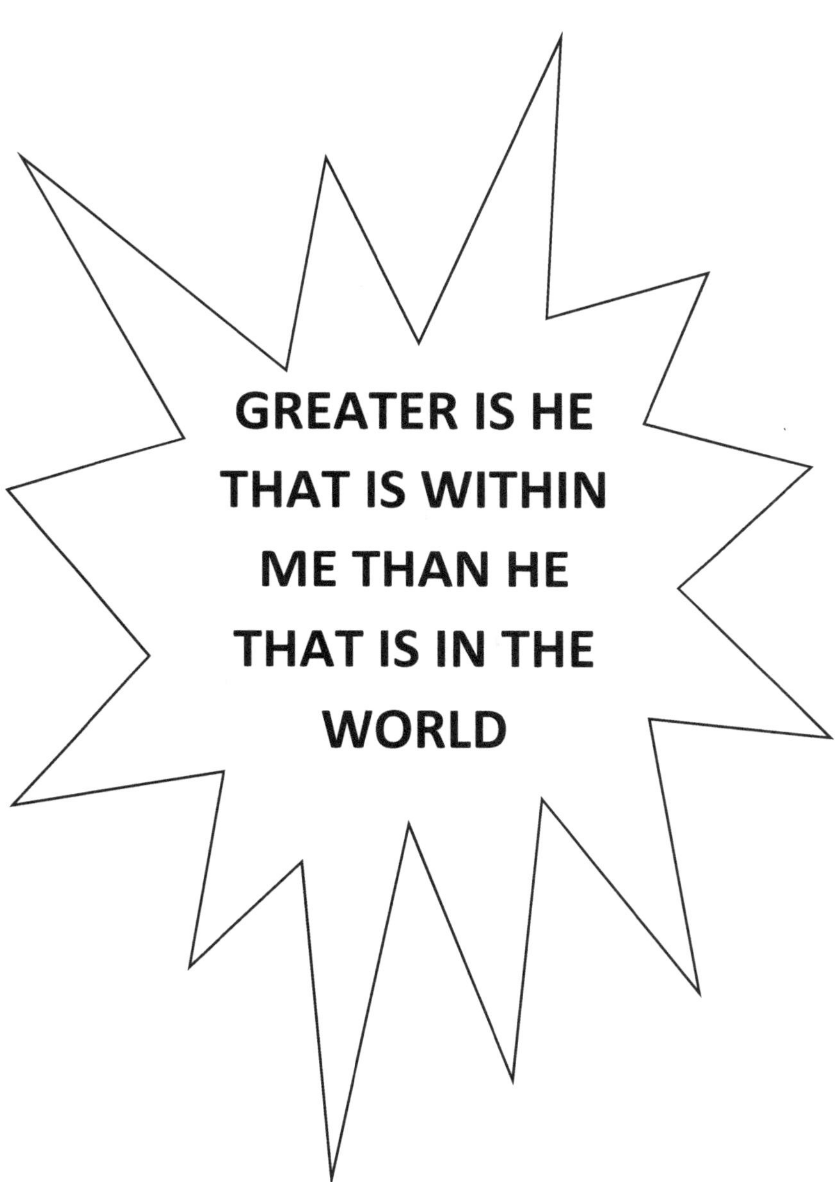


GREATER IS HE
THAT IS WITHIN
ME THAN HE
THAT IS IN THE
WORLD

THE LORD
IS
MY ROCK

I AM AN
OVERCOMER

I CAN DO
IT

I AM THE
HEAD

I CAN
MAKE IT

I AM A
CHILD OF
GOD

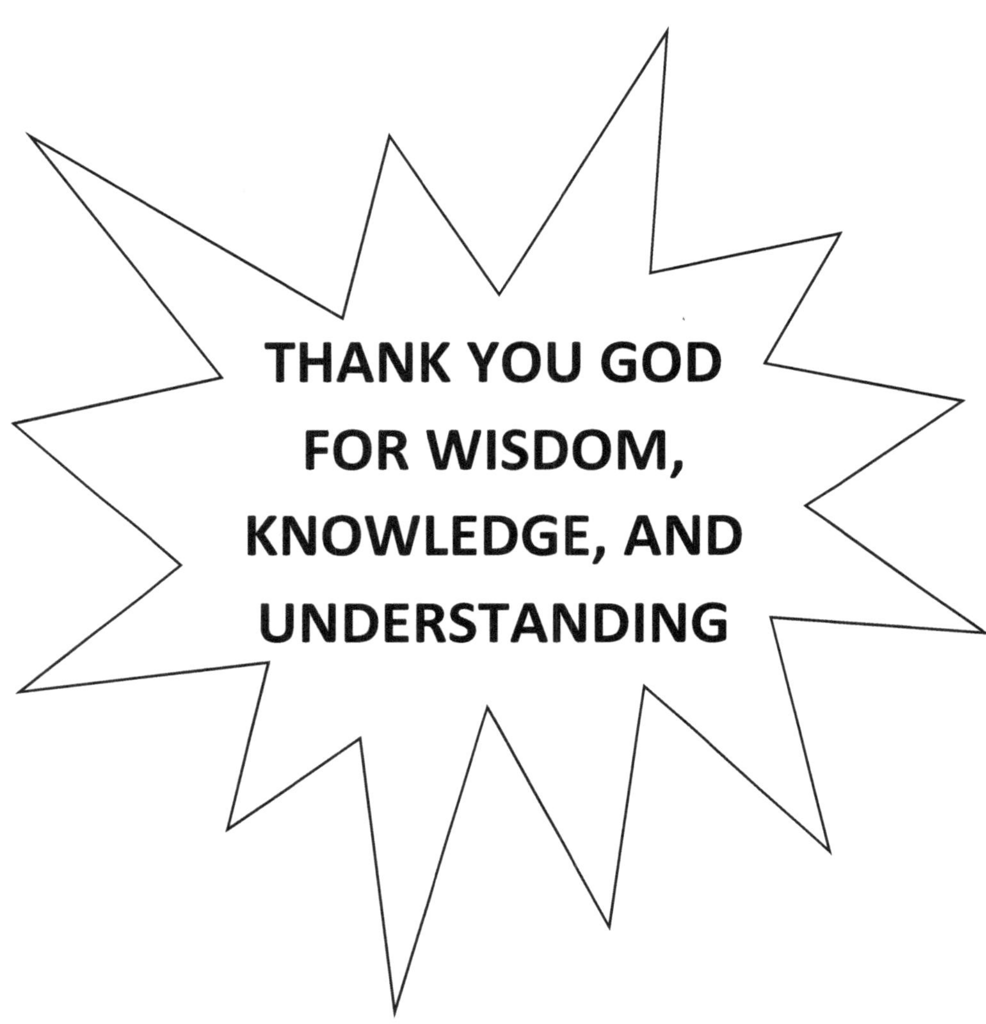

THANK YOU GOD
FOR WISDOM,
KNOWLEDGE, AND
UNDERSTANDING

I AM SAVED BY
THE GRACE OF
GOD

I TRUST IN
THE LORD

I WALK BY
FAITH

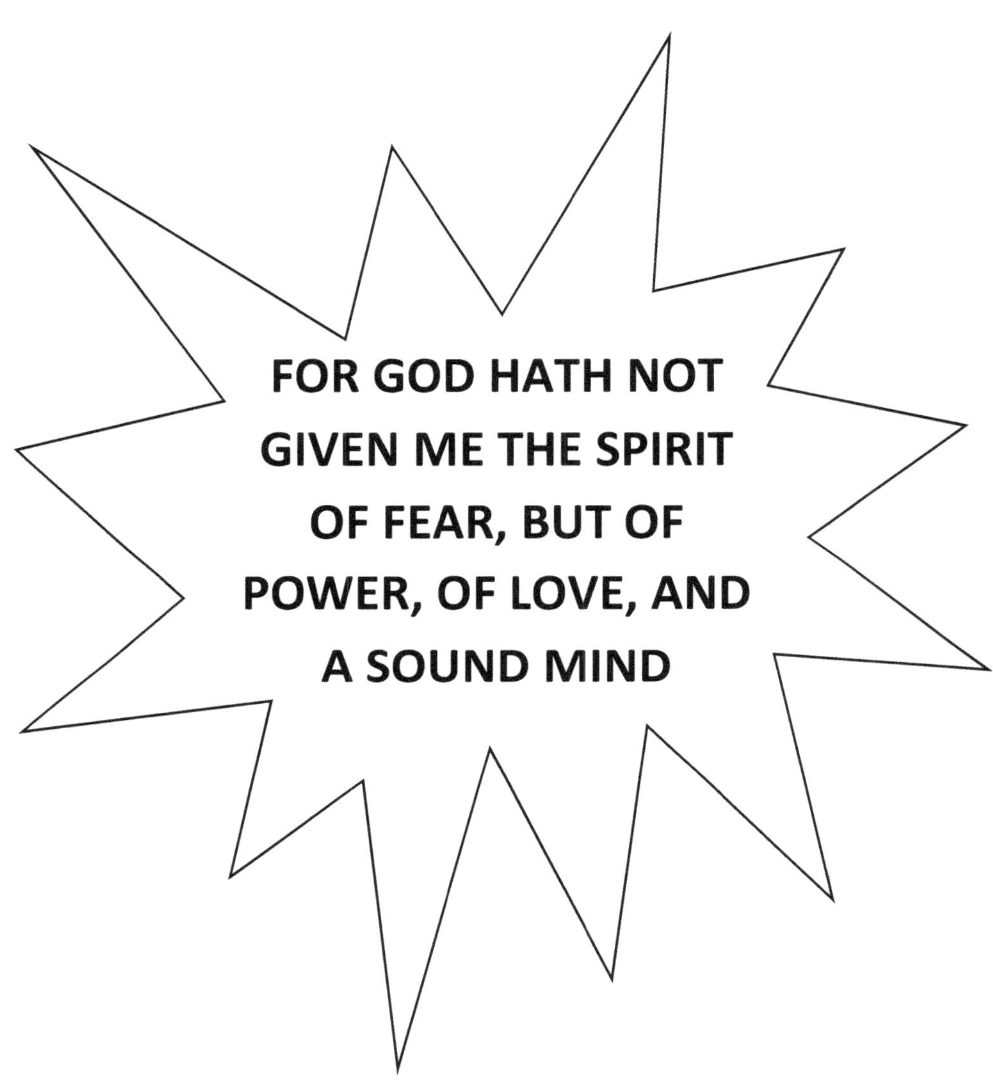


FOR GOD HATH NOT
GIVEN ME THE SPIRIT
OF FEAR, BUT OF
POWER, OF LOVE, AND
A SOUND MIND

THE LORD
IS MY
DELIVERER

MY MIND IS
ALERT

I AM
WHOLE

PRAISE THE
LORD FOR
GOOD HEALTH

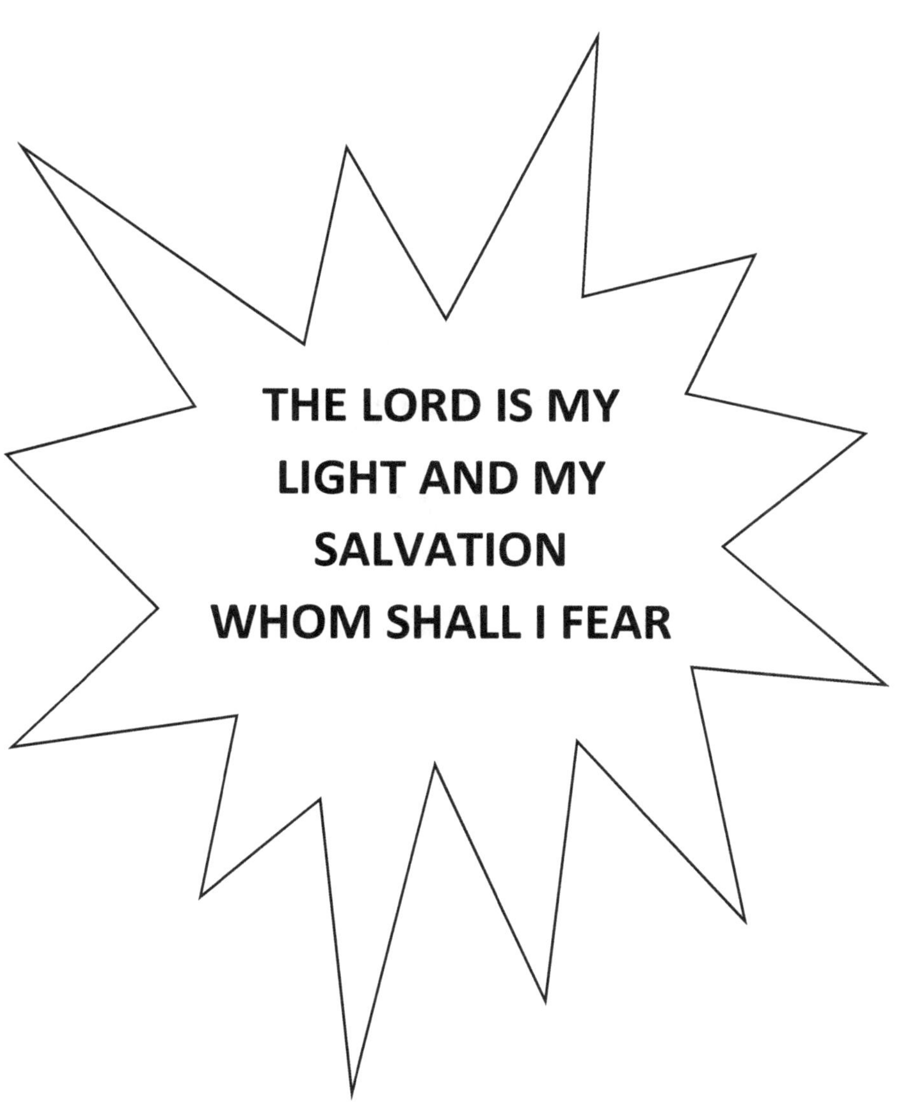

THE LORD IS MY
LIGHT AND MY
SALVATION
WHOM SHALL I FEAR

THE LORD IS
MY
SHEPHERD

I LOVE
YOU
LORD

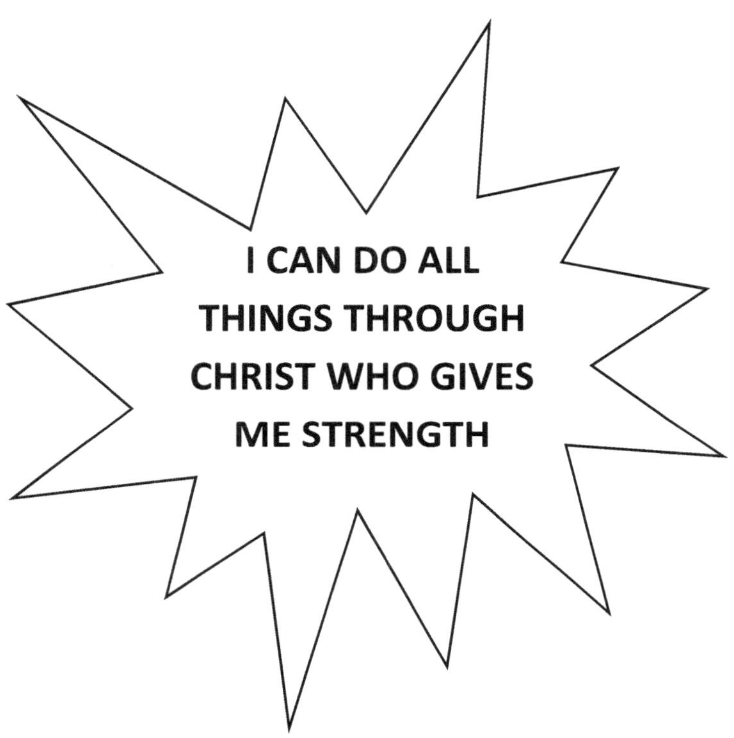

I CAN DO ALL
THINGS THROUGH
CHRIST WHO GIVES
ME STRENGTH

I CHOOSE
TO BE
HAPPY

I HAVE A GOOD
POSITIVE
ATTITUDE

I AM
CONFIDENT

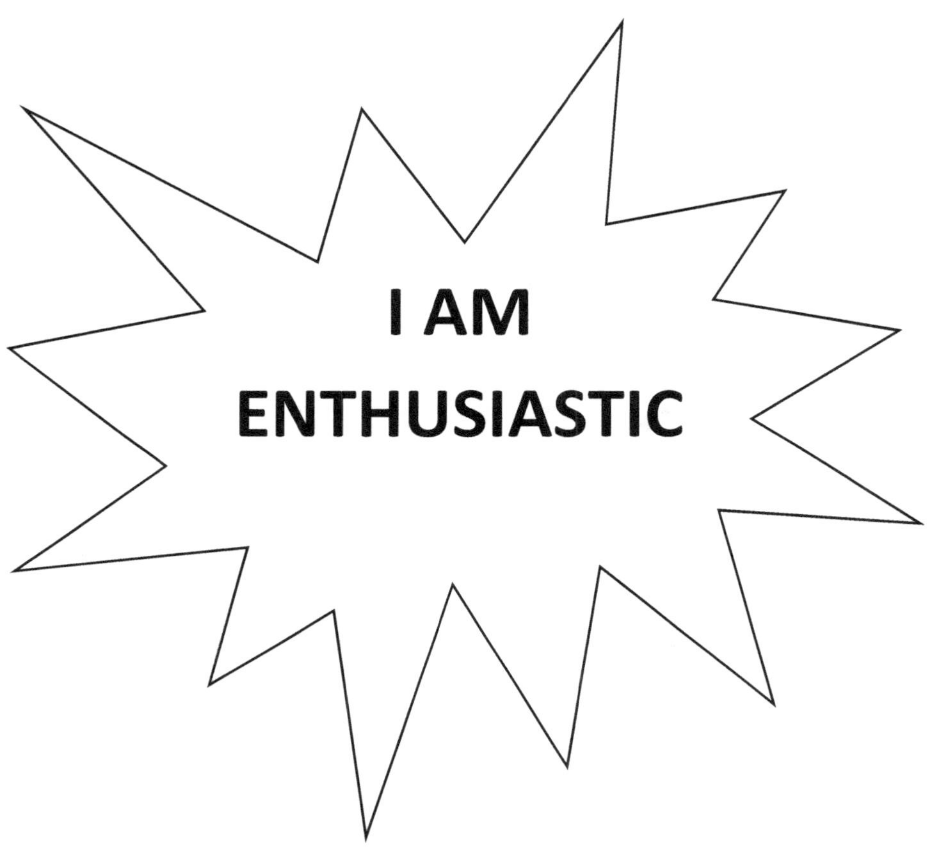

I AM
ENTHUSIASTIC

I AM
CREATIVE

I AM MADE IN
THE IMAGE OF
GOD

I AM A
LEADER

I HAVE
VISION

I HAVE
FORESIGHT

I AM
GRATEFUL

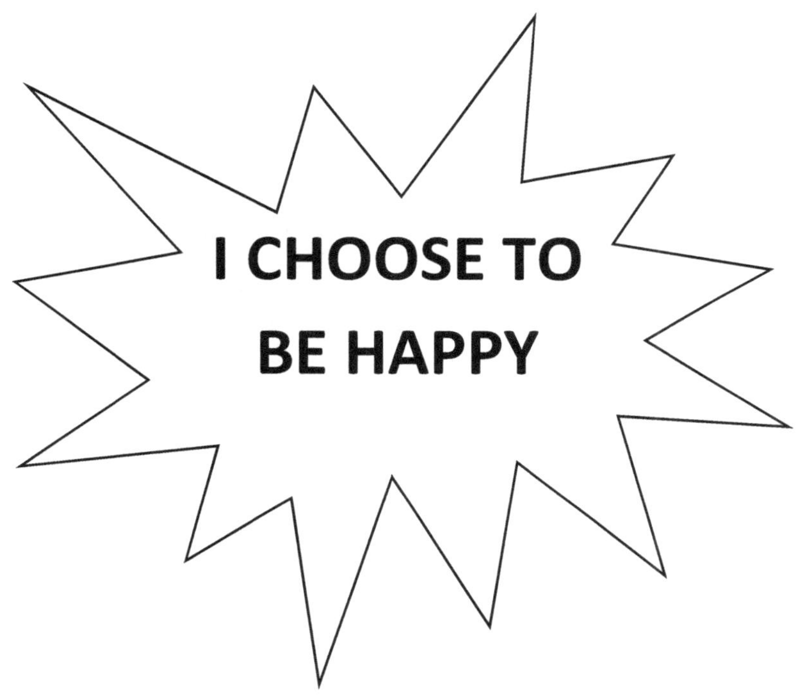
I CHOOSE TO
BE HAPPY

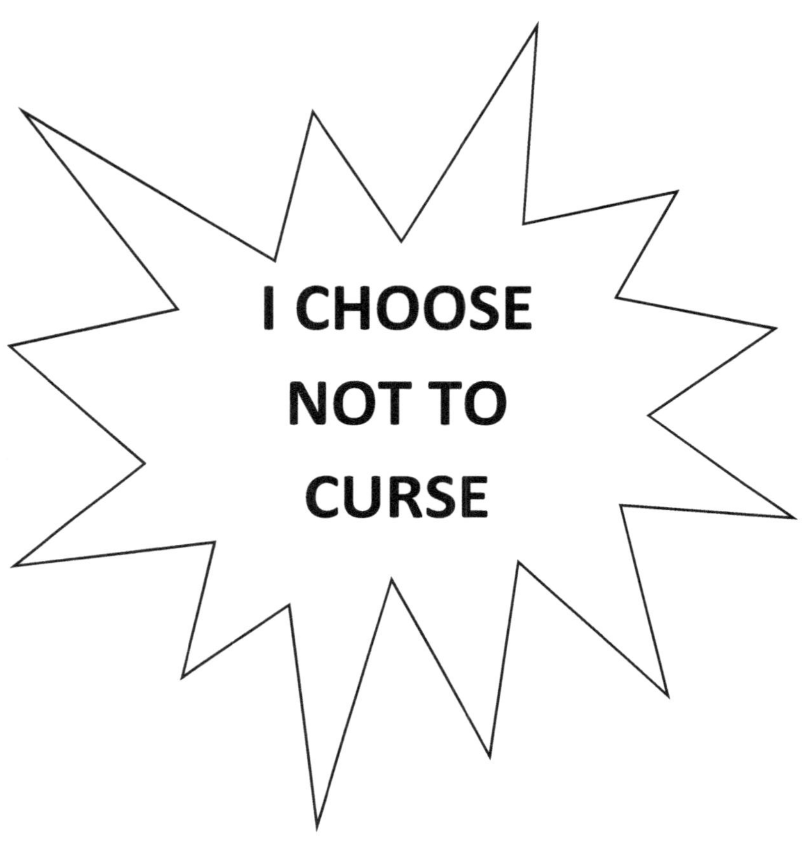

I CHOOSE
NOT TO
CURSE

I SPEAK
GOOD
THINGS

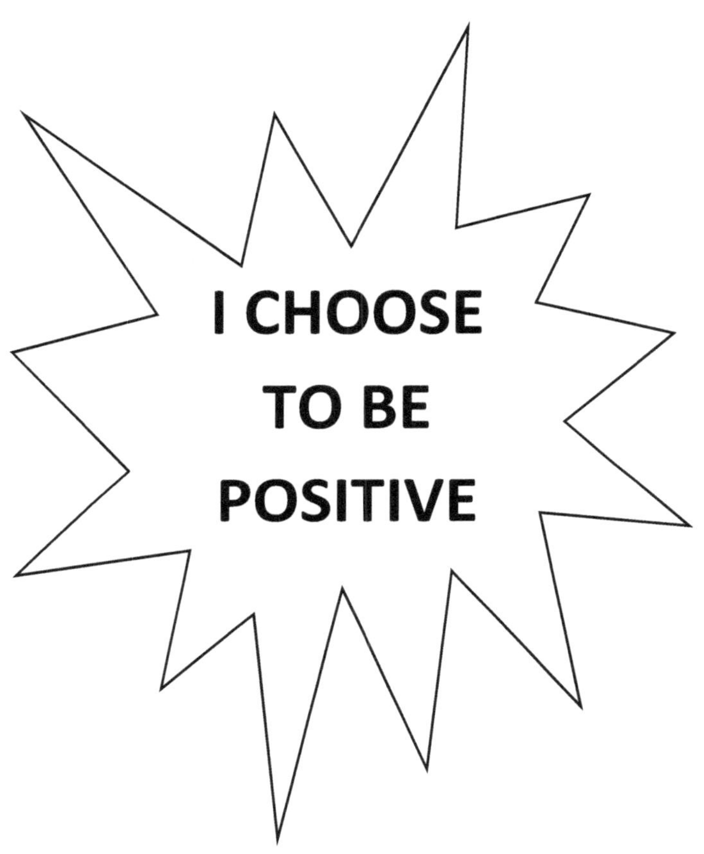
I CHOOSE
TO BE
POSITIVE

I LISTEN TO
GOOD POSITIVE
UPLIFTING
MUSIC

I AM
OPTIMISTIC

I AM
LOVED

# Chapter 11:
# SMART TIPS

<u>Think</u> – *When you are out with your friends, always think for yourself; think and use your own brain. Think and make wise decisions. Your choices and decisions that you make today (good or bad) pave the way for your future.*

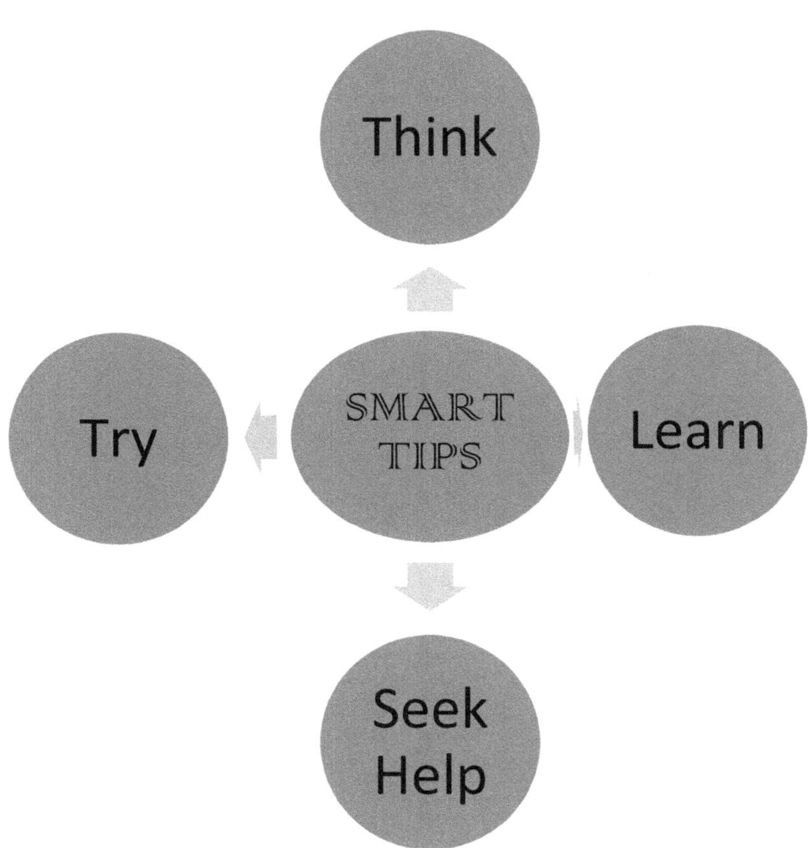
Think
Try
SMART
TIPS
Learn
Seek
Help

# SMART TIPS

<u>Try</u> – *Do not be afraid to try new and worthy things. That is how you grow. Input equals output.  If you do not put anything in do not expect to get anything out.*

<u>Learn</u> – *Make your own mistakes; however, be sure to learn from them so you do not repeat them. Or do not keep repeating them and allowing them to keep you from making progress.*

<u>Seek Help</u> – *Avoid getting into trouble; but if by chance you do, tell your parents, grandparents or guardians immediately so they can help you.*

# ACROSTIC - TIPS

| | |
|---|---|
| **T** | T - Think before you speak or act. |
| **I** | I - Invest your time and money wisely. |
| **P** | P - Pray for your purpose in life. |
| **S** | S - See yourself smart and successful. |

# ACROSTIC - TEENS

| | |
|---|---|
| **T** | T - Time is important, do not take it for granted |
| **E** | E - Education and using it could equate to earning power |
| **E** | E - Enjoy life and have fun |
| **N** | N - Not going to be a Teen forever so make the best of your teen years |
| **S** | S - Save all the money you can |

# ACROSTIC - YOUNG

| | |
|---|---|
| **Y** | Y – Young – youthfulness you will have for a season in life so treasure it |
| **O** | O – Opportunities; seize those that can add value to your life |
| **U** | U – Understanding you should seek along with common sense, knowledge and wisdom |
| **N** | N – Not going to be a Young Adult forever so be wise and make the best of it |
| **G** | G – Grow in GOD read the Bible and pray |

# ACROSTIC - ADULT

| | |
|---|---|
| **A** | A – Access to the finer things in life is a result of having the means to do so |
| **D** | D -Do not give up, always keep trying and one day you will have what you are seeking |
| **U** | U – Use wisdom before you act |
| **L** | L – Love and Learn – Love is a virtue and learn all you can and put it to good use |
| **T** | T – Time waits for no one so manage it |

# Time goes by so fast so......don't waste it

## (Below are things to consider)

- ❖ Always pray and put God first each day.

- ❖ Think good positive thoughts.

- ❖ Smile and speak good things.

- ❖ Set goals.

- ❖ Go for it and do what is morally and legally right to achieve your goals.

- ❖ Do your very best in high school, read and study.

- ❖ There is nothing wrong with getting a tutor.

- ❖ Go to college, technical school or trade school.

❖ Keep trying and never give up on your dreams and pursuits.

❖ Honor your parents.

❖ Always respect and remember your elders.

❖ Travel to places you admire.

❖ Take time to relax and reflect on your life.

❖ Give to others in need.

❖ Always strive to do better.

❖ Be grateful and praise God for blessing you.

❖ Help others achieve their goals when you can.

❖ Do not rush through life.

❖ Take time to enjoy nature and see the beauty in it.

❖ See yourself completing your goals.

❖ Try to get a job you enjoy and it will not seem like work.

❖ Research starting your own business.

❖ Practice speaking good English.

❖ Eat good healthy foods and drinks.

❖ Exercise regularly.

❖ Don't smoke or do drugs; if you have started get help and stop.

❖ Change your friends and peers if they are leading you down the wrong path. You are the company you keep.

❖ Pray and ask God to help you choose good smart friends who are going down the path of legal success.

❖ Take your time and learn new things – new hobbies.

❖ Learn a new sport and if you do not like it, you can always learn a new one.

❖ Laugh often it is good for you.

- ❖ Be friendly and make lots of good friends.

- ❖ Do not be lazy.

- ❖ Learn a foreign language and become fluent in speaking it.

- ❖ Learn how to play an instrument of interest.

- ❖ Learn how to sing it can brighten your day.

- ❖ Learn how to plant flowers and or vegetables.

- ❖ Keep your room clean and help keep other areas in your home clean inside and outside.

- ❖ Plan and set your goals and work towards achieving them.

- ❖ Modify your goals - make necessary changes for the better when you have to.

# Summary

You are embarking life ahead with many choices to make.  After you have read this book, it is my desire that the information contained within has enlightened you.

As a result, I hope it will help you to make wise decisions as you go through life.  Do not get discouraged and become complacent in life.  Seek God first, pray and trust in him to lead you and guide you.  Enjoy the present and make your tomorrows better than your yesterdays, and you will be just fine.

# REFERENCES

Ramsey, Dave (2018). Follow The 7 Steps to Success! Retrieved from https://youtu.be/H2Zd0-0XLBU

The Holy Bible, King James Version.

# ABOUT THE AUTHOR

***Janice Dingle Hunter*** lives by her motto, "*Live and make the most of each day!*" She loves to talk, write, travel, and interact with others.

Her ongoing mission is inspiring others and prompting them to take positive action for desired change.

She has earned a Master degree from Webster University and a Bachelor of Science degree from North Carolina Central University.

Janice is equipped to speak on such topics as *Putting God First; Living the Blessed Life; How to Live Again When All Hope is Gone; Tips for Teens and Young Adults; How to Formulate a Budget and Live; Wealth Building; What is A Virtuous Woman; and LEAP!*

She is available to present on one of the topics listed above <u>or</u> to devise a topic exclusively to fit your next workshop, conference, seminar, or church event.  Book her via email.


<u>*Other Books by the Author or are Coming Soon!*</u>

**Seven Steps to Plan and Prosper**

**Inspirations from the Heart**


Contact Email: swimming4him100@gmail.com

9 781733 197403